Playing v
Pre
Robert Louis Stevensons

Treasure Island
FOR KIDS
(The melodramatic version!)

For 8-25+ actors, or kids of all ages who want to have fun!
Creatively modified by
Brendan P. Kelso
Edited by Khara C. Barnhart
Cover illustrations by Shana Hallmeyer, Ron Leishman, and Adam Watson
Special Contributor: Asif Zamir

3 Melodramatic Modifications of Shakespeare's Play
for 3 different group sizes:

7-9+ actors

10-16+ actors

17-25+ actors

Table Of Contents

Foreword .... Pg 4

School, Afterschool, and Summer classes .... Pg 6

Performance Rights .... Pg 6

7-9+ Actors .... Pg 8

10-16+ Actors .... Pg 32

17-25+ Actors .... Pg 62

Sneak Peeks at other Playing With Plays .... Pg 98

About the Author .... Pg 104

Adam, thanks for hanging out at Starbucks!
- BPK

Playing with Plays™ - Robert Louis Stevenson's Tresure Island for Kids

Copyright © 2004-2020 by Brendan P. Kelso, Playing with Plays LLC
Some characters on the cover are ©Ron Leishman ToonClipart.com

All rights reserved. No part of this book may be reproduced in any form or by any electronic or mechanical means, including photocopying, recording, information storage or retrieval systems now known or to be invented, without permission in writing from the publisher, except by a reviewer, who may quote brief passages in a review, written for inclusion within a periodical. Any members of education institutions wishing to photocopy part or all of the work for classroom use, or publishers who would like to obtain permission to include the work in an anthology, should send their inquiries to the publisher. We monitor the internet for cases of piracy and copyright infringement/violations. We will pursue all cases within the full extent of the law.

Whenever a Playing With Plays play is produced, the following must be included on all programs, printing and advertising for the play: © Brendan P. Kelso, Playing with Plays LLC, www.PlayingWithPlays.com. All rights reserved.

CAUTION: Professionals and amateurs are hereby warned that these plays are subject to a royalty. They are fully protected, in whole, in part, or in any form under the copyright laws of the United States, Canada, the British Empire, and all other countries of the Copyright Union, and are subject to royalty. All rights, including professional, amateur, motion picture, radio, television, recitation, public reading, internet, and any method of photographic reproduction are strictly reserved.

For performance rights please see page 6 of this book or contact:

contact@PlayingWithPlays.com

-Please note, for certain circumstances, we do waive copyright and performance fees. Rules subject to change

www.PlayingWithPlays.com

Printed in the United States of America
Published by Playing With Plays LLC

ISBN: 978-1492194033

ISBN: 1492194034

Foreword

When I was in high school there was something about Shakespeare that appealed to me. Not that I understood it mind you, but there were clear scenes and images that always stood out in my mind. Romeo & Juliet, "Romeo, Romeo; wherefore art thou Romeo?"; Julius Caesar, "Et tu Brute"; Macbeth, "Double, Double, toil and trouble"; Hamlet, "to be or not to be"; A Midsummer Night's Dream, all I remember about this was a wickedly cool fairy and something about a guy turning into a donkey that I thought was pretty funny. It was not until I started analyzing Shakespeare's plays as an actor that I realized one very important thing, I still didn't understand them. Seriously though, it's tough enough for adults, let alone kids. Then it hit me, why don't I make a version that kids could perform, but make it easy for them to understand with a splash of Shakespeare lingo mixed in? And voila! A melodramatic masterpiece was created! They are intended to be melodramatically fun!

THE PLAYS: There are 3 plays within this book, for three different group sizes. The reason: to allow educators or parents to get the story across to their children regardless of the size of their group. As you read through the plays, there are several lines that are highlighted. These are actual lines from the original book. I am a little more particular about the kids saying these lines verbatim. But the rest, well... have fun!

The entire purpose of this book is to instill the love of a classic story, as well as drama, into the kids.

And when you have children who have a passion for something, they will start to teach themselves, with or without school.

These plays are intended for pure fun. Please DO NOT have the kids learn these lines verbatim, that would be a complete waste of creativity. But do have them basically know their lines and improvise wherever they want as long as it pertains to telling the story. Because that is the goal of an actor: to tell the story. In A Midsummer Night's Dream, I once had a student playing Quince question me about one of her lines, "but in the actual story, didn't the Mechanicals state that 'they would hang us'?" I thought for a second and realized that she had read the story with her mom, and she was right. So I let her add the line she wanted and it added that much more fun, it made the play theirs. I have had kids throw water on the audience, run around the audience, sit in the audience, lose their pumpkin pants (size 30 around a size 15 doesn't work very well, but makes for some great humor!) and most importantly, die all over the stage. The kids love it.

One last note: if you want some educational resources, loved our plays, want to tell the world how much your kids loved performing Shakespeare, want to insult someone with our Shakespeare Insult Generator, or are just a fan of Shakespeare, then hop on our website and have fun:

PlayingWithPlays.com

With these notes, I'll see you on the stage, have fun, and break a leg!

SCHOOL, AFTERSCHOOL, and SUMMER classes

I've been teaching these plays as afterschool and summer programs for quite some time. Many people have asked what the program is, therefore, I have put together a basic formula so any teacher or parent can follow and have melodramatic success! As well, many teachers use my books in a variety of ways. You can view the formula and many more resources on my website at: PlayingWithPlays.com

- Brendan

OTHER PLAYS AND FULL LENGTH SCRIPTS

We have over 25 different titles, as well as a full-length play in 4-acts for theatre groups: Shakespeare's Hilarious Tragedies. You can see all of our other titles on our website here: PlayingWithPlays.com/books

As well, you can see a sneak peek at some of those titles at the back of this book.

And, if you ever have any questions, please don't hesitate to ask at: Contact@PlayingWithPlays.com

ROYALTIES

If you have any questions about royalties or performance licenses, here are the basic guidelines:

1) Please contact us! We always LOVE to hear about a school or group performing our books! We would also love to share photos and brag about your program as well! (with your permission, of course)

2) If you are a group and DO NOT charge your kids to be in this production, contact us about discounted copyright fees (one way or another, we will make this work for you!) You are NOT required to buy a book per kid (but, we will still send you some really cool Shakespeare tattoos for your kids!)

3) If you are a group and DO charge your kids to be in the production, (i.e. afterschool program, summer camp) we ask that you purchase a book per kid. Contact us as we will give you a bulk discount (10 books or more) and send some really cool press on Shakespeare tattoos!

4) If you are a group and DO NOT charge the audience to see the plays, please see our website FAQs to see if you are eligible to waive the performance royalties (most performances are eligible).

5) If you are a group and DO charge the audience to see the performance, please see our website FAQs for performance licensing fees (this includes performances for donations and competitions).

Any other questions or comments, please see our website or email us at:

contact@PlayingWithPlays.com

The 15-Minute or so Treasure Island

By Robert Louis Stevenson
Creatively modified by Brendan P. Kelso

7-9+ Actors

CAST OF CHARACTERS:

JIM HAWKINS: Young man of 17, the storyteller

DOCTOR LIVESEY: A doctor who wants to be rich!

SQUIRE TRELAWNEY: A rich man who wants to be richer!

[1]**CAPTAIN SMOLLETT:** Captain of the Hispaniola (a boat)

BEN GUNN: The man of the island

THE PIRATES:

[1]**CAPTAIN BILLY BONES:** A tough old pirate with a map to "The Treasure"

LONG JOHN SILVER: A one-legged pirate, the worst kind!

[2]**PIRATE GEORGE MERRY:** A random pirate

[2]**PIRATE DICK:** Another random pirate

[1]Captain Smollett and Billy Bones can be played by the same actor

[2]Pirate George and Dick can be combined into one Pirate for a cast of 7

Random Pirates and villagers can be extras if needed. (Pirates would, of course, always be saying, "Arrrrghhhh!"

ACT 1 SCENE 1

(enter BILLY and JIM)

BILLY: Fifteen men on the dead man's chest, Yo-ho-ho and a bottle of rum! Hey there, *(addressing JIM)* does this inn get many visitors?

JIM: No, not many at all.

BILLY: Good! Then get me some rum and a room; I'm staying for a while!

(BILLY pulls out his spyglass and looks out the windows nervously, as if he doesn't want to be found)

BILLY: Hey, you, boy! You got a name?

JIM: *(scared)* It's Jim, sir. My father and mother run this inn.

BILLY: I'll give you a silver fourpenny on the first of every month if you keep your eye open for a seafaring man with one leg. They are the worst kind of pirates!

JIM: Deal!

(ALL exit, BILLY is singing Yo-ho-ho)

ACT 1 SCENE 2

(enter JIM addressing audience)

JIM: It's been months now, when is this guy going to leave?! We don't even know his name...

(JIM hears a door knock; JIM exits)

ACT 1 SCENE 3

(enter JIM, holding a piece of paper)

JIM: *(to the audience)* Oh no! *(calling offstage)* Oh, Captain!

(BILLY enters)

BILLY: Who wants me?!?! Arrrrghhh!

JIM: Well some random pirate stopped by and asked for "my mate Bill" and then asked me to give this to you. Oh yeah, and he says you are Captain Billy Bones! *(hands note to BILLY)*

BILLY: *(reading note, then looks at JIM)* Rum! I need Rum! Rum! Ah, man, we have till ten o'clock!

JIM: For what?

BILLY: *(stands up and starts getting really excited)* For what?!?! The Black Spot, that's what! The black spot is a pirates way of saying you're out of the gang! Leave or die!

JIM: That doesn't sound good.

BILLY: *(getting really excited)* We'll get them, yet! Arrrrgghhh!!!! *(grabs his chest)* ...or maybe not! *(then falls to the floor, dead)*

JIM: Captain! Ah, man, now he's dead! What is this random-looking map? *(holding it up for the audience to see)* Must be important, I better show the doctor, he'll know what to do!

(JIM exits dragging CAPTAIN off stage)

ACT 1 SCENE 4

(enter JIM, DOCTOR, and TRELAWNEY)

JIM: Hey, Doctor, and hello Trelawney.

DOCTOR: What's up?

JIM: The Captain is dead.

TRELAWNEY: What! He was the blood-thirstiest buccaneer that sailed.

DOCTOR: Had he money?

TRELAWNEY: Money!?!? Have you heard the story? He had a TREASURE!!! Rumor has it he kept it on an island.

JIM: So, that's why this story is called Treasure Island! And look, here's the map!

(DOCTOR and TRELAWNEY ooooh and ahhhh)

DOCTOR: I can't make head or tail of this.

TRELAWNEY: I can. I'll get a boat and a crew and we will sail for the treasure in three weeks! Cool?

DOCTOR and JIM: Cool!

(ALL exit)

ACT 2 SCENE 1

(enter DOCTOR, TRELAWNEY, and JIM)

DOCTOR: Wow, Trelawney, this is a great ship!

TRELAWNEY: You never imagined a sweeter schooner – the Hispaniola!

(enter SILVER)

TRELAWNEY: I want you to meet someone. This is Long John Silver, our cook!

SILVER: You are our new cabin boy, pleased to meet you! *(very happy and nice and shaking JIM'S hand)*

JIM: *(to audience)* Hey, this guy seems really nice. Can't be the same one-legged guy that Billy Bones warned me about. *(to SILVER)* Hello. I can't help but notice that you only have one leg.

SILVER: Why, shiver my timbers! You seem like a very smart young lad!

TRELAWNEY: See, I told you he was great!

DOCTOR: Let's go in the ship!

(ALL exit)

ACT 2 SCENE 2

(enter JIM, TRELAWNEY, and DOCTOR; enter CAPTAIN SMOLLETT from the other side of the stage)

TRELAWNEY: Hello Captain. Are we all shipshape and seaworthy?

CAPTAIN: Trelawney, I don't know what you're thinking, but I don't like this cruise; and I don't like the men.

TRELAWNEY: *(very angry)* Perhaps you don't like the ship?

CAPTAIN: Nope, I said it short and sweet.

DOCTOR: What? Why?

CAPTAIN: Because I heard we are going on a treasure hunt and the coordinates of the island are: *(whispers to DOCTOR)*

DOCTOR: Wow! That's exactly right!

CAPTAIN: There's been too much blabbing already.

DOCTOR: Right! But, I doubt ANYTHING will go wrong!

CAPTAIN: Fine. Let's sail. But, don't say I didn't warn ya!

(ALL exit)

ACT 2 SCENE 3

(enter JIM, SILVER, and various other pirates)

SILVER: Ay, ay, mates. You know the song: Fifteen men on the dead man's chest.

ALL PIRATES: Yo-ho-ho and a bottle of rum!

(PIRATES slowly exit)

JIM: *(to the audience)* So, the Hispaniola had begun her voyage to the Isle of Treasure. As for Long John, well, he still is the nicest cook...

SILVER: Do you want a sandwich?

JIM: That would be great, thanks, Long John! *(SILVER exits; JIM addresses audience)* As you can see, Long John is a swell guy! Until....

(JIM hides in the corner)

ACT 2 SCENE 4

(enter SILVER and OTHER PIRATES)

JIM: *(to audience)* I overheard Long John talking to the rest of the pirates.

SILVER: Listen here you, Scallywags! I was with Captain Flint when he hid this treasure. And those cowards have the map. Follow my directions, and no killing, yet. Clear?

DICK: Clear.

SILVER: But, when we do kill them, I claim Trelawney. And remember, dead men don't bite.

ALL: Ay, ay, Long John!

(ALL exit but JIM)

JIM: *(to audience)* Oh no! Long John Silver IS the one-legged man that Billy Bones warned me about! I have to tell the others!

(JIM runs offstage)

ACT 2 SCENE 5

(ALL enter)

CAPTAIN: Land ho!

(the PIRATES start cheering)

CAPTAIN: Ok men, go get the ship ready to anchor!

(ALL exit except CAPTAIN, TRELAWNEY, JIM, and DOCTOR)

JIM: Hey guys, we have a slight problem. Long John has secretly rallied the men and they are going to kill us and take our treasure!

TRELAWNEY: Wow, that stinks.

DOCTOR: That Long John is a crafty one!

JIM: Yes.

CAPTAIN: Well, let's act as if we know nothing and we will figure the rest out in the morning. And give them more rum. Rum makes for happy pirates!

OTHERS: Ok!

(ALL exit)

ACT 3 SCENE 1

(enter JIM, SILVER, TRELAWNEY, CAPTAIN, DOCTOR, and various PIRATES)

JIM: *(to audience)* Well, my heart sank into my boots from that first look, I hated the very thought of Treasure Island.

(one side of the stage are THE PIRATES growling and saying a lot of "Arrrrghhs", the other side are the non-pirates)

SILVER: *(to PIRATES)* Men, remember, this is NOT the time to attack.

PIRATES: Ay, ay, Captain!

CAPTAIN: My lads, we've had a hot day. So, as a reward, as many as please can go ashore for the afternoon!

PIRATES: Yeah!!!! *(All PIRATES exit)*

SILVER: *(to audience as he exits)* I'll use this time to get my men in order!

JIM: *(to audience as he runs across stage)* I'm going to shore with them!

DOCTOR: What's Jim doing, going with the pirates!?!?

TRELAWNEY: Got me. He's just a kid, what does he know!

(ALL exit; PIRATES exit on opposite side of good guys)

ACT 3 SCENE 2

(enter JIM, running)

JIM: What was I thinking!? Now that I'm on this island I'm leaving these pirates and going to hide.

(runs offstage)

ACT 3 SCENE 3

(JIM runs on stage, panting; BEN GUNN runs across the stage)

JIM: What was that?! Whether bear, or man, or monkey, I could not tell. But, very quick!

(enter GUNN)

JIM: Who are you?

GUNN: Ben Gunn, matey. I've been on this island for three years!

JIM: Three years! Were you shipwrecked?

GUNN: Nay, mate, marooned with a pistol and a bullet. But, I have survived the island! Who are you hiding from?

JIM: Long John Silver.

GUNN: Blow me down, the pirate with one leg! Ohhh, he's the worst kind of pirate!

JIM: Yes, I'm learning that.

GUNN: Gunn will help you! Let's go find your friends!

(ALL exit)

ACT 4 SCENE 1

(enter DOCTOR, TRELAWNEY, and CAPTAIN)

DOCTOR: We made it to the stockade! Oh no, more pirates behind us, shoot!

(PIRATES enter; everyone shoots and a random PIRATE dies, other PIRATES turn around and run offstage)

TRELAWNEY: Ha, ha! Scared them off!

(everyone moves to one side of the stage; JIM and GUNN enter)

GUNN: Now, there's your friends, sure enough. They are flying the Union Jack flag. Silver would fly the Jolly Roger, make no doubt about that!

JIM: Where are they?

GUNN: In the stockade made years ago by Captain Flint.

JIM: Let's go!

GUNN: No, when Ben Gunn is wanted you know where to find him, Jim.

(GUNN exits)

JIM: *(to audience)* I need to help my friends!

(DOCTOR, SQUIRE, and CAPTAIN enter)

JIM: Doctor! Squire! Captain! Is that you?

DOCTOR: Jim! You're alive!

JIM: Yes! And I met this really cool guy named Ben Gunn, who I don't think has showered in a few years...

(ALL exit)

ACT 4 SCENE 2

(enter TRELAWNEY, DOCTOR, JIM, and CAPTAIN)

DOCTOR: They are waiving the white flag of truce! Keep indoors, men. Ten to one this is a trick. *(calling offstage)* Who goes? Stand, or we fire.

(SILVER enters with GEORGE)

SILVER: Easy there, flag of truce!

CAPTAIN: Look Silver, I don't trust you, plain and simple.

SILVER: It is... simple... you give us the treasure map or we come and kill you.

CAPTAIN: No way! You're a common mutineer and pirate.

SILVER: Okay, then it's nothin' but musket-balls for you!

CAPTAIN: Game on! I'll see you all to Davy Jones Locker!

SILVER: Before an hour's out, I'll be firing upon you. Them that die'll be the lucky ones.

(SILVER and GEORGE exit)

DOCTOR: That went well!

(ALL exit)

ACT 4 SCENE 3

(enter CAPTAIN, JIM, TRELAWNEY, and DOCTOR)

CAPTAIN: Men, we are about to be attacked. If you see someone, shoot!

(shooting breaks out – then stops after a few shots; PIRATES attack; lots of shooting "Bang! Bang!"; then a sword fight breaks out; PIRATES fall over, dead; the rest exit; the CAPTAIN has been injured badly)

JIM: Captain, are you okay?

TRELAWNEY: The captain's wounded.

CAPTAIN: Ehhh, it's just a flesh wound.

(bodies are dragged off as ALL exit)

ACT 5 SCENE 1

(TRELAWNEY, DOCTOR, and CAPTAIN meet off to the side and are discussing something)

TRELAWNEY: Then it's a plan.

DOCTOR: Got it. See ya guys! *(DOCTOR exits)*

JIM: *(to audience)* I think he's going now to see Ben Gunn. I have an idea of my own! I'm going to get our ship! Be right back...

(JIM exits; offstage sounds of gunshots. A random pirate falls on stage and dies. JIM enters and drags body offstage)

JIM: *(to audience)* I got into a small fight, but I'm ok, don't worry. I got our ship back. Now, I have to find my friends at the stockade.

(JIM walks around stage then sees something in the distance)

JIM: Oh look, everyone's asleep. *(starts tip-toeing into the stockade)* I'm just going to sneak in and lie down in my own place like nothing has happened!

(JIM lies down on stage)

ACT 6 SCENE 1

(SILVER, DICK, and GEORGE enter)

SILVER: Who goes?

(JIM lays quietly, hoping nobody notices him)

SILVER: So! Here's Jim Hawkins, shiver my timbers!

GEORGE: Let's kill him!

SILVER: NO! Wait! We can use him as ransom.

GEORGE: *(disappointed)* Fine.

DICK: Silver, we don't like you anymore! We are giving you the...the black spot!

JIM: Not again!

GEORGE: *(a bit scared to be confronting SILVER)* Silver, you have lost our ship, messed up the mutiny, and now you DON'T want to kill this Jim kid. We think you need to step down and no longer lead us. *(DICK agrees with a resounding, "Aaarrrghhhhhh")*

SILVER: I hear ya, but, if I leave, then you are not going to be able to use this! *(holds out the treasure map)*

DICK: You have Captain Flint's treasure map!?!? Well, why didn't you say so! *(happy)* Arrrghhhhhh!!!

SILVER: So, now you're with me? Let's go find the treasure!

(enter DOCTOR)

DOCTOR: I'm here to see the sick.

DICK: Right here, Doc!

GEORGE: Me too!

DOCTOR: *(DOCTOR gives PIRATES medicine, they go away gagging like it's the worst tasting stuff in the world – probably was...)* Well, if it's not Jim.

SILVER: *(pulling DOCTOR aside)* If you want to talk with him, I can arrange it. But, you have to promise to be good to me, if I spare his life. Deal?

DOCTOR: Deal! *(they shake)*

DOCTOR: Hi, Jim.

JIM: Hey, Doctor.

SILVER: *(quickly interrupting)* Okay guys, that's enough! Remember our deal, Doc.

DOCTOR: Yep!

(ALL exit)

ACT 6 SCENE 2

(enter DICK, GEORGE, SILVER, and JIM; SILVER is holding the map)

SILVER: Twenty paces this way. *(PIRATES follow, anxious to find gold)* Seven paces that way... *(reading map)* Tall tree and Spyglass shoulder. What does this all mean?

DICK: *(screams while pointing offstage)* Aghhhhhhh!!!!

GEORGE: Treasure?!?!

DICK: No. A dead body!

(a DEAD BODY suddenly appears on the ground, pointing across stage)

GEORGE: Well, he was a seaman.

SILVER: Ay, ay, Cap'n Flint put him here, he's part of the map and he's pointing the way to the tall tree! Shiver my timbers! Let's go ahead for the doubloons! *(they start walking around the stage as if they are going somewhere. SILVER is reading the map and pointing which way to go as everyone follows)*

SILVER: Ahhhh...this is the spot...

GEORGE: Where's the gold?

DICK: Someone's taken it!

GEORGE: *(getting mad)* Seven hundred thousands pounds of gold is gone!?!?!

SILVER: Shiver me timbers, this is a problem. Jim, take that and stand by for trouble. *(SILVER hands JIM a gun and they slowly move to the other side of the stage)*

JIM: So, you've changed sides again? Back to our side, huh?

SILVER: You betcha, I'm no fool! This is like the very first episode of Survivor!

(DOCTOR and BEN GUNN show up and start shooting pirates; GEORGE and DICK die, the others run into the forest)

DOCTOR: Quick everyone, let's run back to the ship. We have the treasure!

(ALL exit)

ACT 6 SCENE 3

(enter SILVER, DOCTOR, GUNN, CAPTAIN, JIM, and TRELAWNEY; everyone is acting like a ship sailing; ship is leaving Treasure Island)

JIM: I hope I NEVER see that accursed island again! *(pointing offstage)* Oh look, another island, Land ho! Let's go check it out.

(ALL exit except GUNN and SILVER)

SILVER: Ben, you know I have to escape.

GUNN: I know, Silver.

(SILVER runs offstage; DOCTOR, CAPTAIN, JIM, and TRELAWNEY enter)

DOCTOR: Where's Silver?

GUNN: He escaped.

CAPTAIN: Eh, that pirate was nothing but trouble.

JIM: A one-legged pirate, the worst kind!

(ALL exit but JIM)

Epilogue:

JIM: Everyone else got their fair share of the money and did well by it. As for Ben Gunn, he was back on the streets after three weeks, or, to be exact, nineteen days. And as for Silver we have heard no more. And that's how the story ends. Pretty good, huh?

THE END

NOTES

The 20-Minute or so Treasure Island

By Robert Louis Stevenson
Creatively modified by Brendan P. Kelso

10 - 16+ Actors

CAST OF CHARACTERS:

JIM HAWKINS: Young man of 17, the storyteller
DOCTOR LIVESEY: A doctor who wants to be rich!
SQUIRE TRELAWNEY: A rich man who wants to be richer!
CAPTAIN SMOLLETT: Captain of the Hispaniola (a boat)
BEN GUNN: The man of the island
[1]**JIM'S FATHER:** Owner of the Admiral Benbow (bar and inn)
[4]**ABRAHAM GRAY:** A good guy
RANDOM VILLAGERS: Random extras of the village

THE PIRATES:

[4]**CAPTAIN BILLY BONES:** A tough old pirate who has a map to "The Treasure"
LONG JOHN SILVER: A one-legged pirate, the worst kind!
[3]**BLACK DOG:** A pirate
[2]**ISRAEL HANDS:** The first mate
[2]**PEW:** A blind pirate
[1]**PIRATE GEORGE MERRY:** A random pirate
[3]**PIRATE DICK:** Another random pirate
RANDOM PIRATES: Random pirates saying Arrrrghhhh

[1]Jim's Father can also play Pirate George
[2]Israel Hands can also play Pew
[3]Black Dog can also play Pirate Dick
[4]Billy Bones can also play Gray
Random villagers can be anybody not on stage

ACT 1 SCENE 1

(enter BILLY, JIM, and JIM'S FATHER)

BILLY: Fifteen men on the dead man's chest, Yo-ho-ho and a bottle of rum! Hey there, *(addressing JIM'S FATHER)* does this inn get many visitors?

JIM'S FATHER: No, not many at all.

BILLY: Good! Then get me some rum and a room; I'm staying for a while! *(JIM'S FATHER exits)*

(BILLY pulls out his spyglass and looks out the windows nervously, as if he doesn't want to be found)

BILLY: Hey, you, boy! You got a name?

JIM: *(scared)* It's Jim, sir. My father and mother run this inn.

BILLY: I'll give you a silver fourpenny on the first of every month if you keep your eye open for a seafaring man with one leg. They are the worst kind of pirates!

JIM: Deal!

(ALL exit)

ACT 1 SCENE 2

(enter JIM, and RANDOM VILLAGERS who are walking across the stage)

RANDOM VILLAGER 1: *(to another RANDOM VILLAGER 2)* That old pirate's stories are awesome! He is a true sea-dog!

RANDOM VILLAGER 2: Yes, a real old salt! *(RANDOM VILLAGERS exit)*

JIM: *(to audience)* It's been months now, when is this guy going to leave?! We don't even know his name...

(JIM hears a door knock; JIM exits)

ACT 1 SCENE 3

(enter BLACK DOG and JIM from opposite sides of the stage)

BLACK DOG: Come here, sonny. I need to see my mate Bill, he would be called the captain.

JIM: *(to the audience)* Oh no! *(calling offstage)* Oh, Captain!

(BILLY enters)

BILLY: Who wants me?!?! *(sees BLACK DOG)* Arrrrghhh, if it's not Black Dog!

BLACK DOG: And if it's not Captain Billy Bones!

BILLY: Now, look here, you've run me down. Well, then, speak up; what is it?

(BILLY and BLACK DOG continue talking on the side)

JIM: *(to audience)* This guys name is Black Dog and the Captain's is Billy Bones! Cool, huh!

BILLY: *(to BLACK DOG, yelling now)* No, no, no, no; and an end of it!

BLACK DOG: Fine! *(they pull swords and start fighting; BLACK DOG stabs BILLY)*

BILLY: OUCH! That hurt! Take this you scurvy dog! *(stabs BLACK DOG)*

BLACK DOG: *(grabbing his wound)* E-OUCH!!!! I'm outta here! *(runs offstage)*

BILLY: *(yelling offstage)* And be gone with ya! *(looks at JIM)* Rum! I need Rum! Rum! Arrrrgh, this hurts! I need to sleep!

(ALL exit)

ACT 1 SCENE 4

(enter PEW and JIM)

PEW: My name is Pew, take me to the captain.

JIM: *(to the audience)* Aw, man, not another one! And "Pew", what's up with these names?! *(yelling offstage)* Oh, Captain! There's some blind pirate looking for you!

(BILLY enters looking ill)

BILLY: Now what?

PEW: Here ya go, the black spot. And now that's done. *(PEW exits)*

BILLY: Ah, man, we have till ten o'clock!

JIM: For what?

BILLY: *(stands up and starts getting really excited)* For what?!?! The Black Spot, that's what! The black spot is a pirates way of saying you're out of the gang! Leave or die!

JIM: That doesn't sound good.

BILLY: *(getting really excited)* We'll get them, yet! Arrrrgghhh!!!! *(grabs his chest)* ...or maybe not! *(then falls to the floor, dead)*

JIM: Captain! Ah, man, now he's dead! What is this random-looking map? *(holding it up for the audience to see)* Must be important, I better show the doctor, he'll know what to do!

JIM: Oh no, here come some pirates! *(JIM hides)*
(enter BLACK DOG and PEW)
PEW: Down with the door!
BLACK DOG: Captain Bill's dead!
PEW: Search him and his room!
BLACK DOG: The money's there, but not the map.
PEW: Arrrrrrrgh!!!!!!!! I hear the police, run!
(ALL exit)

ACT 1 SCENE 6

(enter JIM, DOCTOR, and TRELAWNEY)

JIM: Hey, Doctor, and hello Trelawney.

DOCTOR: What's up?

JIM: The Captain is dead.

TRELAWNEY: What! He was the blood-thirstiest buccaneer that sailed.

DOCTOR: Had he money?

TRELAWNEY: Money!?!? Have you heard the story? He had a TREASURE!!! Rumor has it he kept it on an island.

JIM: So, that's why this story is called Treasure Island! And look, here's the map!

(DOCTOR and TRELAWNEY ooooh and ahhhh)

DOCTOR: I can't make head or tail of this.

TRELAWNEY: I can. I'll get a boat and a crew and we will sail for the treasure in three weeks! Cool?

DOCTOR and JIM: Cool!

(ALL exit)

ACT 2 SCENE 1

(enter DOCTOR, TRELAWNEY, and JIM)

DOCTOR: Wow, Trelawney, this is a great ship!

TRELAWNEY: You never imagined a sweeter schooner – the Hispaniola!

(enter SILVER)

TRELAWNEY: I want you to meet someone. This is Long John Silver, our cook!

SILVER: You are our new cabin boy, pleased to meet you! *(very happy and nice and shaking JIM'S hand)*

JIM: *(to audience)* Hey, this guy seems really nice. Can't be the same one-legged guy that Billy Bones warned me about. *(to SILVER)* Hello. I can't help but notice that you only have one leg.

SILVER: Why, shiver my timbers! You seem like a very smart young lad!

TRELAWNEY: See, I told you he was great!

DOCTOR: Let's go in the ship!

(ALL exit)

ACT 2 SCENE 2

(enter JIM, TRELAWNEY, and DOCTOR; enter CAPTAIN SMOLLETT from the other side of the stage)

TRELAWNEY: Hello Captain. Are we all shipshape and seaworthy?

CAPTAIN: Trelawney, I don't know what you're thinking, but I don't like this cruise; and I don't like the men.

TRELAWNEY: *(very angry)* Perhaps you don't like the ship?

CAPTAIN: Nope, I said it short and sweet.

DOCTOR: What? Why?

CAPTAIN: Because I heard we are going on a treasure hunt and the coordinates of the island are: *(whispers to DOCTOR)*

DOCTOR: Wow! That's exactly right!

CAPTAIN: There's been too much blabbing already.

DOCTOR: Right! But, I doubt ANYTHING will go wrong!

CAPTAIN: Fine. Let's sail!

(ALL exit)

ACT 2 SCENE 3

(enter JIM, SILVER, and various other pirates)

SILVER: Ay, ay, mates. You know the song: Fifteen men on the dead man's chest.

ALL PIRATES: Yo-ho-ho and a bottle of rum!

(PIRATES slowly exit)

JIM: *(to the audience)* So, the Hispaniola had begun her voyage to the Isle of Treasure. As for Long John, well, he still is the nicest cook…

SILVER: Do you want a sandwich?

JIM: That would be great, thanks, Long John! *(SILVER exits; JIM addresses audience)* As you can see, Long John is a swell guy! Until….

(JIM hides in the corner)

ACT 2 SCENE 4

(enter SILVER and OTHER PIRATES)

JIM: *(to audience)* I overheard Long John talking to the rest of the pirates.

SILVER: Listen here you, Scallywags! I was with Captain Flint when he hid this treasure. And those cowards have the map. Follow my directions, and no killing, yet. Clear?

DICK: Clear.

SILVER: But, when we do kill them, I claim Trelawney. And remember, dead men don't bite.

ALL: Ay, ay, Long John!

(ALL exit but JIM)

JIM: *(to audience)* Oh no! Long John Silver IS the one-legged man that Billy Bones warned me about! I have to tell the others!

(JIM runs offstage)

ACT 2 SCENE 5

(ALL enter)

CAPTAIN: Land ho!

(the PIRATES start cheering)

CAPTAIN: Ok men, go get the ship ready to anchor!

(ALL exit except CAPTAIN, TRELAWNEY, JIM, and DOCTOR)

JIM: Hey guys, Long John has secretly rallied the men and they are going to kill us and take our treasure!

TRELAWNEY: Wow, that stinks.

DOCTOR: That Long John is a crafty one!

JIM: Yes.

CAPTAIN: Well, let's act as if we know nothing and we will figure the rest out in the morning. And give them more rum. Rum makes for happy pirates!

OTHERS: Ok!

(ALL exit)

ACT 3 SCENE 1

(enter JIM, SILVER, TRELAWNEY, CAPTAIN, DOCTOR, and various PIRATES)

JIM: *(to audience)* Well, my heart sank into my boots from that first look, I hated the very thought of Treasure Island.

(one side of the stage are THE PIRATES growling and saying a lot of "Arrrrghhs", the other side are the non-pirates)

SILVER: *(to PIRATES)* Men, remember, this is NOT the time to attack.

PIRATES: Ay, ay, Captain!

CAPTAIN: My lads, we've had a hot day. So, as a reward, as many as please can go ashore for the afternoon!

PIRATES: Yeah!!!! *(All PIRATES exit)*

SILVER: *(to audience as he exits)* I'll use this time to get my men in order!

JIM: *(to audience as he runs across stage)* I'm going to shore with them!

DOCTOR: What's Jim doing, going with the pirates!?!?

TRELAWNEY: Got me. He's just a kid, what does he know!

(ALL exit; PIRATES exit on opposite side of good guys)

ACT 3 SCENE 2

(enter JIM, running)

JIM: What was I thinking!? Now that I'm on this island I'm leaving these pirates and going to hide.

(runs offstage)

ACT 3 SCENE 3

(JIM runs on stage, panting; BEN GUNN runs across the stage)

JIM: What was that?! Whether bear, or man, or monkey, I could not tell. But, very quick!

(enter GUNN)

JIM: Who are you?

GUNN: Ben Gunn, matey. I've been on this island for three years!

JIM: Three years! Were you shipwrecked?

GUNN: Nay, mate, marooned with a pistol and a bullet. But, I have survived the island! Who are you hiding from?

JIM: Long John Silver.

GUNN: Blow me down, the pirate with one leg! Ohhh, he's the worst kind of pirate!

JIM: Yes, I'm learning that.

GUNN: Gunn will help you! Let's go find your friends!

(ALL exit)

ACT 4 SCENE 1

(enter DOCTOR, CAPTAIN, and TRELAWNEY)

CAPTAIN: Men, we have to abandon ship. Pack the food and guns on the little jolly boat and let's go!

(enter ISRAEL HANDS, ABRAHAM GRAY, and other PIRATES)

CAPTAIN: Pirates, we are leaving this boat. And if any one of you make a signal to your "friends" on land. I'll shoot ya!

PIRATES: *(angrily)* Arrrrghhhhhh!!!!

CAPTAIN: It's to you, Abraham Gray. I know you are a good man at bottom. Join me.

ABRAHAM: I'm with you, sir. I hate rum anyway! *(the PIRATES swing their swords at ABRAHAM and miss as he joins the CAPTAIN)*

(ALL exit)

ACT 4 SCENE 2

(enter DOCTOR, TRELAWNEY, CAPTAIN, and ABRAHAM)

DOCTOR: We made it to the stockade! Oh no, more pirates behind us, shoot!

(PIRATES enter; everyone shoots and a random PIRATE dies, other PIRATES turn around and run offstage)

TRELAWNEY: Ha, ha! Scared them off!

(everyone moves to one side of the stage; JIM and GUNN enter)

GUNN: Now, there's your friends, sure enough. They are flying the Union Jack flag. Silver would fly the Jolly Roger, make no doubt about that!

JIM: Where are they?

GUNN: In the stockade made years ago by Captain Flint.

JIM: Let's go!

GUNN: No, when Ben Gunn is wanted you know where to find him, Jim. *(GUNN exits)*

JIM: *(to audience)* I need to help my friends!

(DOCTOR, SQUIRE, and CAPTAIN enter)

JIM: Doctor! Squire! Captain! Is that you?

DOCTOR: Jim! You're alive!

JIM: Yes! And I met this really cool guy named Ben Gunn, who I don't think has showered in a few years...

(ALL exit)

ACT 4 SCENE 3

(enter TRELAWNEY, ABRAHAM, DOCTOR, JIM, and CAPTAIN)

DOCTOR: They are waiving the white flag of truce! Keep indoors, men. Ten to one this is a trick. *(calling offstage)* Who goes? Stand, or we fire.

(SILVER enters with GEORGE)

SILVER: Easy there, flag of truce!

CAPTAIN: Look Silver, I don't trust you, plain and simple.

SILVER: It is... simple... you give us the treasure map or we come and kill you.

CAPTAIN: No way! You're a common mutineer and pirate.

SILVER: Okay, then it's nothin' but musket-balls for you!

CAPTAIN: Game on! I'll see you all to Davy Jones locker!

SILVER: Before an hour's out, I'll be firing upon you. Them that die'll be the lucky ones.

(SILVER and GEORGE exit)

DOCTOR: That went well!

(ALL exit)

ACT 4 SCENE 4

(enter CAPTAIN, JIM, TRELAWNEY, and DOCTOR)

CAPTAIN: Men, we are about to be attacked. If you see someone, shoot!

(shooting breaks out – then stops after a few shots; PIRATES attack; lots of shooting "Bang! Bang!"; then a sword fight breaks out; PIRATES fall over, dead; the rest exit; the CAPTAIN has been Injured badly)

JIM: Captain, are you okay?

TRELAWNEY: The captain's wounded.

CAPTAIN: Ehhh, it's just a flesh wound.

(bodies are dragged off as ALL exit)

ACT 5 SCENE 1

(ABRAHAM, TRELAWNEY, DOCTOR, and CAPTAIN meet off to the side and are discussing something)

TRELAWNEY: Then it's a plan.

DOCTOR: Got it. See ya guys! *(DOCTOR exits)*

ABRAHAM: Is Doctor Livesey mad?

JIM: No. I think he's going now to see Ben Gunn. *(to audience)* I have an idea of my own! I'm going to take Ben Gunn's coracle, that's a small boat for you that don't know, and get our ship back!

(ALL exit)

ACT 5 SCENE 2

(JIM enters; HANDS is asleep on stage)

JIM: *(to audience)* Well, I just set this ship adrift by cutting the anchor.

(HANDS wakes up)

HANDS: Who goes there?

JIM: It's me, Isreal Hands, and I'm taking the ship, nothing personal!

HANDS: Ay, ay, cap'n Hawkins. *(gets up and salutes JIM; points offstage)* Oh, look, land!

JIM: Where?

HANDS: *(attacks JIM)* Right here.

(they fight, JIM kills HANDS)

JIM: Get your hands off me!

(JIM exits and drags HANDS offstage)

ACT 5 SCENE 3

(enter JIM, breathing heavily)

JIM: *(to audience)* OK, now that I have run this ship ashore in a safe harbor, I've got to find my friends at the stockade.

(JIM walks around stage then sees something in the distance)

JIM: Oh look, everyone's asleep. *(starts tip-toeing into the stockade)* I'm just going to sneak in and lie down in my own place like nothing has happened!

(JIM lies down on stage)

ACT 6 SCENE 1

(SILVER, DICK, and GEORGE enter)

SILVER: Who goes?

(JIM lays quietly, hoping nobody notices him)

SILVER: So! Here's Jim Hawkins, shiver my timbers!

GEORGE: Let's kill him!

SILVER: NO! Wait! We can use him as ransom.

GEORGE: *(disappointed)* Fine.

DICK: Silver, we don't like you anymore! We are giving you...the black spot!

JIM: Not again!

GEORGE: *(a bit scared to be confronting SILVER)* Silver, you have lost our ship, messed up the mutiny, and now you DON'T want to kill this Jim kid. We think you need to step down and no longer lead us. *(DICK agrees with a resounding, "Aaarrrghhhhhh")*

SILVER: I hear ya, but, if I leave, then you are not going to be able to use this! *(holds out the treasure map)*

DICK: You have Captain Flint's treasure map!?!? Well, why didn't you say so! *(happy)* Arrrghhhhhh!!!

SILVER: So, now you're with me? Let's go find the treasure!

(enter DOCTOR)

DOCTOR: I'm here to see the sick.

DICK: Right here, Doc!

GEORGE: Me too!

DOCTOR: *(DOCTOR gives PIRATES medicine, they go away gagging like it's the worst tasting stuff in the world – probably was...)* Well, if it's not Jim.

SILVER: *(pulling DOCTOR aside)* If you want to talk with him, I can arrange it. But, you have to promise to be good to me, if I spare his life. Deal?

DOCTOR: Deal! *(they shake)*

DOCTOR: Hi, Jim.

JIM: Hey, Doctor.

SILVER: *(quickly interrupting)* Okay guys, that's enough! Remember our deal, Doc.

DOCTOR: Yep!

(ALL exit)

ACT 6 SCENE 2

(enter DICK, GEORGE, SILVER, and JIM; SILVER is holding the map)

SILVER: Twenty paces this way. *(PIRATES follow, anxious to find gold)* Seven paces that way... *(reading map)* Tall tree and Spyglass shoulder. What does this all mean?

DICK: *(screams while pointing offstage)* Aghhhhhhh!!!!

GEORGE: Treasure?!?!

DICK: No. A dead body!

(a DEAD BODY suddenly appears on the ground, pointing across stage)

GEORGE: Well, he was a seaman.

SILVER: Ay, ay, Cap'n Flint put him here, he's part of the map and he's pointing the way to the tall tree! Shiver my timbers! Let's go ahead for the doubloons! *(they start walking around the stage as if they are going somewhere. SILVER is reading the map and pointing which way to go as everyone follows)*

SILVER: Ahhhh...this is the spot...

GEORGE: Where's the gold?

DICK: Someone's taken it!

GEORGE: *(getting mad)* Seven hundred thousands pounds of gold is gone!?!?!

SILVER: Shiver me timbers, this is a problem. Jim, take that and stand by for trouble. *(SILVER hands JIM a gun and they slowly move to the other side of the stage)*

JIM: So, you've changed sides again? Back to our side, huh?

SILVER: You betcha, I'm no fool! This is like the very first episode of Survivor!

(DOCTOR and BEN GUNN show up and start shooting pirates; GEORGE and DICK die, the others run into the forest)

DOCTOR: Quick everyone, let's run back to the ship. We have the treasure!

(ALL exit)

ACT 6 SCENE 3

(enter SILVER, DOCTOR, GUNN, CAPTAIN, JIM, and TRELAWNEY; everyone is acting like a ship sailing; ship is leaving Treasure Island)

JIM: I hope I NEVER see that accursed island again! *(pointing offstage)* Oh look, another island, Land ho! Let's go check it out.

(ALL exit except GUNN and SILVER)

SILVER: Ben, you know I have to escape.

GUNN: I know, Silver.

(SILVER runs offstage; DOCTOR, CAPTAIN, JIM, and TRELAWNEY enter)

DOCTOR: Where's Silver?

GUNN: He escaped.

CAPTAIN: Eh, that pirate was nothing but trouble.

JIM: A one-legged pirate, the worst kind!

(ALL exit but JIM)

Epilogue:

JIM: Everyone else got their fair share of the money and did well by it. As for Ben Gunn, he was back on the streets after three weeks, or, to be exact, nineteen days. And as for Silver we have heard no more. And that's how the story ends. Pretty good, huh?

THE END

NOTES

The 25-Minute or so Treasure Island

By Robert Louis Stevenson
Creatively modified by Brendan P. Kelso

17 - 25+ Actors

CAST OF CHARACTERS:

JIM HAWKINS: Young man of 17, the storyteller
DOCTOR LIVESEY: A doctor who wants to be rich!
SQUIRE TRELAWNEY: A rich man who wants to be richer!
CAPTAIN SMOLLETT: Captain of the Hispaniola (a boat)
BEN GUNN: The man of the island
[5]**JIM'S FATHER:** Owner of the Admiral Benbow (bar and inn)
[6]**JIM'S MOTHER:** Jim's mom
[1]**MR. DANCE:** An officer
[3]**ABRAHAM GRAY:** A good guy
[5]**TOM REDRUTH:** Another good guy
[6]**HUNTER:** And another good guy
JOYCE: Yes, and another good guy
RANDOM VILLAGERS: Random extras of the village

THE PIRATES:

[3]**CAPTAIN BILLY BONES:** A tough old pirate who has a map to "The Treasure"

LONG JOHN SILVER: A one-legged pirate, the worst kind!

[4]**BLACK DOG:** A pirate

[8]**MR. ARROW:** The ships first, first mate

[2]**ISREAL HANDS:** The ships second, first mate

PARROT: Long John Silver's parrot

[2]**PEW:** A blind pirate

[7]**PIRATE O'BRIEN:** A pirate that wears a red nightcap.

PIRATE GEORGE MERRY: A random pirate

[4]**PIRATE DICK:** Another random pirate

[1]**PIRATE TOM MORGAN:** And another random pirate

[8]**PIRATE JOHNNY:** Yep, another random pirate!

RANDOM PIRATES: Random pirates saying Arrrrghhhh

[7]**A DEAD BODY:** It's a dead body.

[1] Mr. Dance can play Pirate Morgan
[2] Isreal Hands can also play Pew
[3] Billy Bones can also play Grey
[4] Black Dog can also play Pirate Dick
[5] Jim's Father can also play Tom
[6] Jim's mother can also play Hunter
[7] O'brien can also play the dead body
[8] Mr. Arrow can also play Pirate Johnny

Part I - The Old Buccaneer
ACT 1 SCENE 1
The Old Sea-dog at the Admiral Benbow

(enter BILLY, JIM, JIM'S FATHER, and RANDOM VILLAGER carrying some of Billy Bone's stuff)

BILLY: Fifteen men on the dead man's chest, Yo-ho-ho and a bottle of rum! Hey there, *(addressing JIM'S FATHER)* does this inn get many visitors?

JIM'S FATHER: No, not many at all.

BILLY: Good! Then get me some rum and a room; I'm staying for a while! *(RANDOM VILLAGER and JIM'S FATHER exit)*

(BILLY pulls out his spyglass and looks out the windows nervously, as if he doesn't want to be found)

BILLY: Hey, you, boy! You got a name?

JIM: *(scared)* It's Jim, sir. My father and mother run this inn.

BILLY: Come here.

JIM: Yes?

BILLY: I'll give you a silver fourpenny on the first of every month if you keep your eye open for a seafaring man with one leg.

JIM: Deal! *(to the audience)* That's easy money!

BILLY: *(yelling)* Remember! The seafaring man with one leg! They are the worst kind of pirates!

JIM: Deal!

(ALL exit)

ACT 1 SCENE 2
Black Dog Appears and Disappears

(enter JIM'S FATHER, JIM'S MOTHER, JIM, BILLY, and RANDOM VILLAGERS enjoying a night at the Tavern)

BILLY: Arrrhhhh, I remember a night when I got in a fight with these island people... *(he carries on his story to everyone in the background)*

JIM'S MOTHER: *(to JIM'S FATHER)* He scares everyone with his dreadful stories!

JIM'S FATHER: I know, but he scares me with that dreadful cutlass swinging under his coat!

JIM'S MOTHER: What's a cutlass?

JIM'S FATHER: A sword! Shhhhhhhh!!!!!!

RANDOM VILLAGER 1: *(to another RANDOM VILLAGER 2)* I love these stories! This guy is a true sea-dog!

RANDOM VILLAGER 2: Yes, a real old salt!

JIM'S MOTHER: It's been months now, when is this guy going to leave?! We don't even know his name...

(ALL exit)

ACT 1 SCENE 3
The Black Spot

(enter BLACK DOG and JIM from opposite sides of the stage)

BLACK DOG: Come here, sonny.

JIM: Can I help you, sir?

BLACK DOG: I need to see my mate Bill.

JIM: *(to the audience)* I hope he doesn't mean The Captain! *(to Black Dog)* Sir, I don't know your mate Bill.

BLACK DOG: Sure ya do, my mate Bill would be called the captain.

JIM: *(to the audience)* Oh no! *(calling offstage)* Oh, Captain!

(BILLY enters)

BILLY: Who wants me?!?! *(sees BLACK DOG)* Arrrrghhh, if it's not Black Dog!

BLACK DOG: And if it's not Captain Billy Bones!

BILLY: Now, look here, you've run me down. Well, then, speak up; what is it?

(enter JIM'S MOTHER. BILLY and BLACK DOG continue talking on the side)

JIM'S MOTHER: *(to JIM)* Who is that, and what does he want?

JIM: Got me, but his name is Black Dog. Cool, huh!

BILLY: *(to BLACK DOG, yelling now)* No, no, no, no; and an end of it!

BLACK DOG: Fine! *(they pull swords and start fighting; BLACK DOG stabs BILLY)*

BILLY: OUCH! That hurt! Take this you rat-eating seadog! *(stabs BLACK DOG)*

BLACK DOG: *(grabbing his wound)* E-OUCH!!!! I'm outta here! *(runs offstage)*

BILLY: *(yelling offstage)* And be gone with ya! *(looks at JIM)* Rum! I need Rum! Rum!

JIM'S MOTHER: Dear, dear me! What a disgrace upon the house! *(yells out)* You scurvy pirates!

BILLY: Arrrrgh, this hurts! I need to sleep!

(ALL exit)

ACT 1 SCENE 4

The Sea-Chest

(enter PEW and JIM)

PEW: *(to JIM)* Take me to the captain.

JIM: *(to the audience)* Aw, man, not another one! And "Pew", what's up with these names?! *(yelling offstage)* Oh, Captain! There's some blind pirate looking for you!

(BILLY enters looking ill)

BILLY: Now what?

PEW: Here ya go, the black spot. And now that's done. *(PEW exits)*

BILLY: Ah, man, we have till ten o'clock!

JIM: For what?

BILLY: *(stands up and starts getting really excited)* For what?!?! The Black Spot, that's what! The black spot is a pirates way of saying you're out of the gang! Leave or die!

JIM: That doesn't sound good.

BILLY: *(getting really excited)* We'll get them, yet! Arrrrgghhh!!!! *(grabs his chest)* ...or maybe not! *(then falls to the floor, dead)*

JIM: Captain! Ah, man, now he's dead! *(calling offstage)* Mom!

(enter JIM'S MOTHER)

JIM'S MOTHER: *(screams)* Aghhhhhhh!!!!!!!! He didn't even pay me!!!!!

JIM: Mom, the other pirates will be back soon.

JIM'S MOTHER: Well, then, I want my money. Search him and his chest!

JIM: There's a random-looking map. *(holding it up for the audience to see)* Must be important.

JIM'S MOTHER: You better show the doctor, he'll know what to do!

(ALL exit except BILLY)

ACT 1 SCENE 5

The Last of the Blind Man

(enter JIM'S MOTHER and JIM hiding in a corner of the stage)

JIM: *(to audience)* My curiosity, in a sense, was stronger than my fear. *(to JIM'S MOTHER)* Mom, I have to stay and watch.

JIM'S MOTHER: Oh, dear! *(she faints)*

JIM: Fainted...Hmmm, well, at least she'll be quiet. Oh no, here come some more pirates! *(JIM hides)*

(enter BLACK DOG, JOHNNY, and PEW)

PEW: Down with the door!

BLACK DOG: Captain Bill's dead!

PEW: Search him and his room!

JOHNNY: The money's there, but not the map.

PEW: Arrrrrrrgh!!!!!!!!! Here come the police, run!

(PIRATES run around stage. Enter MR. DANCE galloping like he is on a horse, accidentally tramples PEW to death, other PIRATES exit)

MR. DANCE: Whoops! *(to JIM)* Anyway, where are the rest of those pirates!?

JIM: They ran off that way!

MR. DANCE: What in fortune were they after?

JIM: This! I think.

(shows the map, ALL exit)

ACT 1 SCENE 6
The Captain's Papers

(enter JIM, DOCTOR, and TRELAWNEY)

JIM: Hey, Doctor, and hello Trelawney.

DOCTOR: What's up?

JIM: The Captain is dead.

TRELAWNEY: What! He was the blood-thirstiest buccaneer that sailed.

DOCTOR: Had he money?

TRELAWNEY: Money!?!? Have you heard the story? He had a TREASURE!!! Rumor has it he kept it on an island.

JIM: So, that's why this story is called Treasure Island! And look, here's the map!

(DOCTOR and TRELAWNEY ooooh and ahhhh)

DOCTOR: I can't make head or tail of this.

TRELAWNEY: I can. I'll get a boat and a crew and we will sail for the treasure in three weeks! Cool?

DOCTOR and JIM: Cool!

(ALL exit)

Part II – The Sea-Cook
ACT 2 SCENE 1
I Go to Bristol and At the Sign of the "Spy-Glass"

(enter DOCTOR, TRELAWNEY, and JIM)

DOCTOR: Wow, Trelawney, this is a great ship!

TRELAWNEY: You never imagined a sweeter schooner – the Hispaniola!

(enter SILVER)

TRELAWNEY: I want you to meet someone. This is Long John Silver, our cook!

SILVER: You are our new cabin boy, pleased to meet you! *(very happy and nice and shaking JIM'S hand)*

JIM: *(to audience)* Hey, this guy seems really nice. Can't be the same one-legged guy that Billy Bones warned me about. *(to SILVER)* Hello. I can't help but notice that you only have one leg.

SILVER: Why, shiver my timbers! You seem like a very smart young lad!

TRELAWNEY: See, I told you he was great!

DOCTOR: Let's go in the ship!

(ALL exit)

ACT 2 SCENE 2

Powder and Arms

(enter MR. ARROW, JIM, TRELAWNEY, and DOCTOR)

TRELAWNEY: Mr. Arrow, we are looking for Captain Smollett.

MR. ARROW: I will take you to him right away. *(yells offstage)* Oh, Captain!

(enter CAPTAIN SMOLLETT)

TRELAWNEY: Hello Captain. Are we all shipshape and seaworthy?

CAPTAIN: Trelawney, I don't know what you're thinking, but I don't like this cruise; I don't like the men and I don't like my officer. *(pointing at MR. ARROW)*

(MR. ARROW makes a loud "hmfffp" sound and exits)

TRELAWNEY: *(very angry)* Perhaps you don't like the ship?

CAPTAIN: Nope, I said it short and sweet.

DOCTOR: What? Why?

CAPTAIN: Because the deckhands that YOU hired know more about where we are going than I DO!

JIM: What have you heard?

CAPTAIN: That we are going on a treasure hunt and the coordinates of the island are: *(whispers to DOCTOR)*

DOCTOR: Wow! That's exactly right!

CAPTAIN: There's been too much blabbing already.

DOCTOR: Right! But, I doubt ANYTHING will go wrong!

CAPTAIN: Fine. Let's sail. But, don't say I didn't warn ya!

(ALL exit)

ACT 2 SCENE 3

The Voyage

(enter SILVER, JIM, and various other pirates)

SILVER: Ay, ay, mates. You know the song: Fifteen men on the dead man's chest.

ALL PIRATES: Yo-ho-ho and a bottle of rum!

(ALL slowly exit as Jim goes through his speech)

JIM: *(to the audience)* So, the Hispaniola had begun her voyage to the Isle of Treasure. It turns out that Mr. Arrow was worse than the captain had feared. And, well...somehow he "fell overboard" during the cruise. *(some pirates throw MR. ARROW offstage, like they are throwing him overboard "OVERBOARD!" is yelled from offstage)* As for Long John, well, he still is the nicest cook. Curiously, he has a parrot named...

(enter SILVER with his PARROT)

SILVER: Cap'n Flint, after the famous buccaneer.

PARROT: Pieces of eight! Pieces of eight! Pieces of eight!

JIM: What are 'pieces of eight'?

SILVER: Ay, it's gold, matey! Do you want a sandwich?

JIM: That would be great, thanks, Long John! *(SILVER exits; JIM addresses audience)* As you can see, Long John is a swell guy! Until....

(JIM hides in the corner)

ACT 2 SCENE 4
What I Heard in the Apple Barrel

(enter SILVER and OTHER PIRATES)

JIM: *(to audience)* I overheard Long John talking to the rest of the pirates.

SILVER: Listen here you, Scallywags! I was with Captain Flint when he hid this treasure. And those cowards have the map!

RANDOM PIRATE: When we get to the island, can we kill them then?

SILVER: No, you will follow my directions, clear?

DICK: Clear.

SILVER: But, when we do kill them, I claim Trelawney. And remember, dead men don't bite.

ALL: Ay, ay, Long John!

(ALL exit but JIM)

JIM: *(to audience)* Oh no! Long John Silver IS the one-legged man that Billy Bones warned me about! I have to tell the others!

(JIM runs offstage)

ACT 2 SCENE 5
Council of War

(ALL enter)

CAPTAIN: Land ho!

(the PIRATES start cheering)

CAPTAIN: Has any one of you seen that land ahead?

SILVER: I have, sir. It's called Skeleton Island. And we called that inlet 'Captain Kidd's Anchorage'.

CAPTAIN: Ok men, go get the ship ready to anchor!

(ALL exit except CAPTAIN, TRELAWNEY, JIM, and DOCTOR)

JIM: Hey guys, we have a slight problem.

DOCTOR: What's that?

JIM: Um, Long John has secretly rallied the men and they are going to kill us and take our treasure!

TRELAWNEY: Wow, that stinks.

DOCTOR: That Long John is a crafty one!

JIM: Yes.

CAPTAIN: Well, let's act as if we know nothing and we will figure the rest out in the morning. And give them more rum. Rum makes for happy pirates!

OTHERS: Ok!

(ALL exit)

Part III - My Shore Adventure
ACT 3 SCENE 1
How My Shore Adventure Began

(enter JIM, SILVER, TRELAWNEY, CAPTAIN, DOCTOR, and various PIRATES)

JIM: *(to audience)* Well, my heart sank into my boots from that first look, I hated the very thought of Treasure Island.

(one side of the stage are THE PIRATES growling and saying a lot of "Arrrrghhs", the other side are the non-pirates)

SILVER: *(to PIRATES)* Men, remember, this is NOT the time to attack.

PIRATES: Ay, ay, Captain!

CAPTAIN: My lads, we've had a hot day. So, as a reward, as many as please can go ashore for the afternoon!

PIRATES: Yeah!!!! *(All PIRATES exit)*

SILVER: *(to audience as he exits)* I'll use this time to get my men in order!

JIM: *(to audience as he runs across stage)* I'm going to shore with them!

DOCTOR: What's Jim doing, going with the pirates!?!?

TRELAWNEY: Got me. He's just a kid, what does he know!

(ALL exit; PIRATES exit on opposite side of good guys)

ACT 3 SCENE 2

The First Blow

(enter JIM, running)

JIM: What was I thinking!? Now that I'm on this island I'm leaving these pirates and going to hide. *(JIM hides in corner of stage; enter PIRATES and SILVER with swords out)*

SILVER: Men, we are going to take the treasure my way, is that clear?

TOM: NO, I won't hurt them, they are nice people.

SILVER: You're either with us......... or dead.

TOM: Right, I guess you'll have to kill me if you can. *(starts to leave)*

SILVER: OK, I'm good with that.

(SILVER stabs TOM in the back)

TOM: Ah man, really?

(TOM dies melodramatically)

SILVER: Anyone else? *(silence)* Good. Let's go!

(ALL exit, they drag TOM offstage)

JIM: Well, he just killed an honest man! Ahhhh, I'm next!!!!

(runs offstage)

ACT 3 SCENE 3

The Man of the Island

(JIM runs on stage, panting; BEN GUNN runs across the stage)

JIM: What was that?! Whether bear, or man, or monkey, I could not tell. But, very quick!

(enter GUNN)

JIM: Who are you?

GUNN: Ben Gunn, matey. I've been on this island for three years!

JIM: Three years! Were you shipwrecked?

GUNN: Nay, mate, marooned with a pistol and a bullet. But, I have survived the island! Who are you hiding from?

JIM: Long John Silver.

GUNN: Not the man...with one...leg?

JIM: Yep!

GUNN: Blow me down! Ohhh, he's the worst kind of pirate!

JIM: Yes, I'm learning that.

GUNN: Gunn will help you! Let's go find your friends!

(ALL exit)

Part IV - The Stockade
ACT 4 SCENE 1
How the Ship was Abandoned

(enter DOCTOR, REDRUTH, CAPTAIN, and TRELAWNEY)

CAPTAIN: Men, pack the food and guns on the little jolly boat and let's go!

REDRUTH: You got it, Cap'n!

(enter ISREAL HANDS, ABRAHAM GRAY, and other PIRATES)

CAPTAIN: Pirates, we are leaving this boat. And if any one of you make a signal to your "friends" on land. I'll shoot ya!

PIRATES: *(angrily)* Arrrrghhhhhh!!!!

CAPTAIN: It's to you, Abraham Gray. I know you are a good man at bottom. Join me.

ABRAHAM: I'm with you, sir. I hate rum anyway! *(the PIRATES swing their swords at ABRAHAM and miss as he joins the CAPTAIN)*

(ALL exit)

ACT 4 SCENE 2

The Jolly-Boat's Last Trip

(enter REDRUTH, DOCTOR, CAPTAIN, TRELAWNEY, and ABRAHAM all bunched together as if on a tiny boat)

REDRUTH: Cap'n, this little boat we are in and rowing to shore, is starting to take on water.

CAPTAIN: Oh, no! Look back at the ship, they are using the long nine!

DOCTOR: Aghhhhhhh!!!!! What's the "long nine"?

ABRAHAM: It's a cannon, and it's being fired by Isreal Hands; he was Flint's gunner.

CAPTAIN: Who's the best shot, here?

TRELAWNEY: I am, sir!

CAPTAIN: Great. Pick me off one of those men, sir.

TRELAWNEY: Ok! *(he aims and fires)* Got one! *(a random PIRATE runs on stage and dies melodramatically)*

DOCTOR: Uh, oh! Incoming! Duck!

REDRUTH: We've been hit and the boat's sinking! Luckily, we're in three feet of water, let's run for it!

(ALL exit)

ACT 4 SCENE 3
End of the First Day's Fighting

(enter REDRUTH, DOCTOR, TRELAWNEY, JOYCE, HUNTER, CAPTAIN, and ABRAHAM)

DOCTOR: We made it to the stockade! Oh no, more pirates behind us, shoot!

(PIRATES enter; everyone shoots and a random PIRATE dies, other PIRATES turn around and run offstage)

TRELAWNEY: Ha, ha! Scared them off!

(shots fired offstage)

CAPTAIN: Duck! They are firing at us!

(REDRUTH is hit and dies melodramatically)

HUNTER: Well, that stinks!

CAPTAIN: Quick, in the stockade!

(ALL exit)

ACT 4 SCENE 4

The Garrison in the Stockade

(JIM and GUNN enter)

GUNN: Now, there's your friends, sure enough.

JIM: How do you know?

GUNN: They are flying the Union Jack flag. Silver would fly the Jolly Roger, make no doubt about that!

JIM: Where are they?

GUNN: In the stockade made years ago by Captain Flint.

JIM: Let's go!

GUNN: No, when Ben Gunn is wanted you know where to find him, Jim. *(GUNN exits)*

JIM: *(to audience)* I need to help my friends!

(DOCTOR, SQUIRE, and CAPTAIN enter)

JIM: Doctor! Squire! Captain! Is that you?

DOCTOR: Jim! You're alive!

JIM: Yes! And I met this really cool guy named Ben Gunn, who I don't think has showered in a few years…

(ALL exit)

ACT 4 SCENE 5
Silver's Embassy
The Attack

(enter HUNTER, JOYCE, TRELAWNEY, ABRAHAM, DOCTOR, JIM, and CAPTAIN)

HUNTER: They are waiving the white flag of truce!

JOYCE: It's Silver himself!

DOCTOR: Keep indoors, men. Ten to one this is a trick. *(calling offstage)* Who goes? Stand, or we fire.

(SILVER enters with GEORGE)

SILVER: Easy there, flag of truce!

CAPTAIN: Look Silver, I don't trust you, plain and simple.

SILVER: It is... simple... you give us the treasure map or we come and kill you.

CAPTAIN: No way! You're a common mutineer and pirate.

SILVER: Okay, then it's nothin' but musket-balls for you!

CAPTAIN: Game on! I'll see you all to Davy Jones locker!

SILVER: Before an hour's out, I'll be firing upon you. Them that die'll be the lucky ones.

(SILVER and GEORGE exit)

DOCTOR: That went well!

CAPTAIN: Men, we are about to be attacked. If you see someone, shoot!

(shooting breaks out – then stops after a few shots)

CAPTAIN: Did you hit your man?

JOYCE: No sir.

(PIRATES attack; lots of shooting "Bang! Bang!"; two PIRATES fall over, dead; the rest exit; then more PIRATES enter and attack; HUNTER gets hit and falls over, dead; a swordfight breaks out; more PIRATES get killed and so does JOYCE; the CAPTAIN has been injured badly)

JIM: Captain, are you okay?

TRELAWNEY: The captain's wounded.

CAPTAIN: Ehhh, it's just a flesh wound.

(bodies are dragged off as ALL exit)

Part V - My Sea Adventure
ACT 5 SCENE 1
How My Sea Adventure Began

(TRELAWNEY, DOCTOR, and CAPTAIN meet off to the side and are discussing something)

TRELAWNEY: Then it's a plan.

DOCTOR: Got it. See ya guys! *(DOCTOR exits)*

ABRAHAM: Is Doctor Livesey mad?

JIM: No. I think he's going now to see Ben Gunn. *(to audience)* I have an idea of my own! I'm going to take Ben Gunn's coracle, that's a small boat for you that don't know, and get our ship back! *(acts like he is rowing on stage)*

JIM: Ah, ha! There's the ship. Ahhh man, they're two pirates on the ship; Israel Hands and O'Brien. What am I to do?

(JIM's off to the side watching as HANDS and O'BRIEN enter arguing and fighting)

O'BRIEN: Is too!

HANDS: Is not!

O'BRIEN: Is TOO!

HANDS: Is NOT!

(they swordfight and HANDS is stabbed but O'BRIEN is killed; JIM exits)

HANDS: IS NOT! *(to audience)* Wow, I'm suddenly tired.

(HANDS falls asleep and stays on stage)

ACT 5 SCENE 2
The Ebb-Tide Runs
The Cruise of the Coracle
I Strike the Jolly Roger
Israel Hands

(JIM enters; HANDS is asleep on stage)

JIM: *(to audience)* Well, I just set this ship adrift by cutting the anchor.

(HANDS wakes up)

HANDS: Who goes there?

JIM: It's me, Isreal Hands, and I'm taking the ship, nothing personal!

HANDS: Ay, ay, cap'n Hawkins. *(gets up and salutes JIM; points offstage)* Oh, look, land!

JIM: Where?

HANDS: *(attacks JIM)* Right here.

(they fight, JIM kills HANDS)

JIM: Get your hands off me!

(JIM exits and drags HANDS offstage)

ACT 5 SCENE 3

Pieces of Eight

(enter JIM, breathing heavily)

JIM: *(to audience)* Man, those bodies are heavier than I thought! OK, I've got to find my friends at the stockade.

(JIM walks around stage then sees something in the distance)

JIM: Oh look, everyone's asleep. *(starts tip-toeing into the stockade)* I'm just going to sneak in and lie down in my own place like nothing has happened!

PARROT: Pieces of eight! Pieces of Eight! Pieces of Eight! *(continues for a short while)*

JIM: *(shocked)* What the.... NOOOOOOOO... it's Silver's green parrot, Captain Flint!

(JIM lies down on stage)

Part VI - Captain Silver
ACT 6 SCENE 1
In the Enemy's Camp
The Black Spot Again

(SILVER and other PIRATES enter)

SILVER: Who goes?

(JIM lays quietly, hoping nobody notices him)

SILVER: So! Here's Jim Hawkins, shiver my timbers!

GEORGE: Let's kill him!

SILVER: NO! Wait! We can use him as ransom.

GEORGE: *(disappointed)* Fine.

DICK: Silver, we don't like you anymore! Pirates, let's talk outside!

(ALL exit except JIM and SILVER)

JIM: What are they doing? Cause, I'm with you, I don't want to be killed.

SILVER: Ahhh, they're going to give me the black spot.

JIM: Not again!

(PIRATES enter)

MORGAN: *(scared to confront SILVER)* Silver, you have lost our ship, messed up the mutiny, and now you DON'T want to kill this Jim kid. We think you need to step down and no longer lead us. *(Other pirates agree with a resounding, "Aaarrrghhhhhh")*

SILVER: I hear ya, but, if I leave, then you are not going to be able to use this! *(holds out the treasure map)*

DICK: You have Captain Flint's treasure map!?!? Well, why didn't you say so!

PIRATES: *(happy)* Arrrghhhhhh!!!

SILVER: So, now you're with me? Let's go find the treasure!

(ALL exit)

ACT 6 SCENE 2

On Parole

(enter DOCTOR, PIRATES, SILVER, and JIM)

DOCTOR: I'm here to see the sick.

DICK: Right here, Doc!

GEORGE: Me too!

DOCTOR: *(DOCTOR gives PIRATES medicine, they go away gagging like it's the worst tasting stuff in the world – probably was…)* Well, if it's not Jim.

SILVER: *(pulling DOCTOR aside)* If you want to talk with him, I can arrange it. But, you have to promise to be good to me, if I spare his life. Deal?

DOCTOR: Deal! *(they shake)*

(DOCTOR and JIM are off to the side)

DOCTOR: What happened?

JIM: I got the ship!

DOCTOR: Sweet! We will get it ready for sailing.

JIM: Great! And I'll work on staying alive!

DOCTOR: Great!

(SILVER approaches)

SILVER: *(quickly interrupting)* Okay guys. Remember our deal, Doc.

DOCTOR: Yep!

(ALL exit)

ACT 6 SCENE 3

The Treasure Hunt – Flint's Pointer

(enter PIRATES, SILVER, and JIM; SILVER is holding the map)

SILVER: Twenty paces this way. *(PIRATES follow, anxious to find gold)* Seven paces that way... *(reading map)* Tall tree and Spyglass shoulder. What does this all mean?

DICK: *(screams while pointing offstage)* Aghhhhhhh!!!!

MORGAN: Treasure?!?!

DICK: No. A dead body!

(a DEAD BODY suddenly appears on the ground, pointing across stage)

GEORGE: Well, he was a seaman.

SILVER: Ay, ay, Cap'n Flint put him here, he's part of the map and he's pointing the way to the tall tree! Shiver my timbers! Let's go ahead for the doubloons!

(they start walking around the stage as if they are going somewhere; ALL remain onstage)

ACT 6 SCENE 4
The Treasure Hunt – The Voice Among the Trees
The Fall of a Chieftain

GUNN: *(a ghost-like voice from offstage)* Fifteen men on a dead man's chest, Yo-ho-ho and a bottle of rum!

MORGAN: What was that!?!?!?

MERRY: It's a ghost! Captain Flint's back from the dead!

DICK: I'm scared. *(the PIRATES look scared)*

SILVER: Get a hold of yourselves!

GUNN: *(as voice)* Darby M'Graw. Darby M'Graw. Darby M'Graw!

MORGAN: They was Flint's last words!!!

(PIRATES run around stage screaming and running into each other)

SILVER: *(yelling)* STOP!!!! *(PIRATES stop and look at SILVER)* I'm here to get that gold, and no one dead or alive is going to stop me! Let's go!

(SILVER is reading the map and pointing which way to go as everyone follows)

SILVER: Ahhhh...this is the spot...

MERRY: Where's the gold?

DICK: Someone's taken it!

MORGAN: *(getting mad)* Seven hundred thousands pounds of gold is gone!?!?!

SILVER: Shiver me timbers, this is a problem. Jim, take that and stand by for trouble. *(SILVER hands JIM a gun and they slowly move to the other side of the stage)*

JIM: So, you've changed sides again? Back to our side, huh?

SILVER: You betcha, I'm no fool! This is like the very first episode of Survivor!

(DOCTOR, GRAY, and BEN GUNN show up and start shooting pirates; GEORGE and DICK die, the others run into the forest)

DOCTOR: Quick everyone, let's run back to the ship. We have the treasure!

(ALL exit)

ACT 6 SCENE 7
And Last

(enter SILVER, DOCTOR, GUNN, CAPTAIN, JIM, and TRELAWNEY)

DOCTOR: You're the man to keep your word, Silver.

SILVER: As are you, Doctor.

TRELAWNEY: So what do you want, Silver?

SILVER: Just don't leave me stranded on the island and take me back to England for my punishment.

CAPTAIN: You're a prodigious villain and impostor, but, deal. Let's sail!

(on stage everyone is acting like a ship sailing.)

JIM: I hope I NEVER see that accursed island again! Oh look, another island, Land ho! An actual island with actual people. Let's go check it out.

(ALL exit except GUNN and SILVER)

SILVER: Ben, you know I have to escape.

GUNN: I know, Silver.

(SILVER runs offstage; DOCTOR, CAPTAIN, JIM, and TRELAWNEY enter)

DOCTOR: Where's Silver?

GUNN: He escaped.

CAPTAIN: Eh, that pirate was nothing but trouble.

JIM: A one-legged pirate, the worst kind!

(ALL exit but JIM)

Epilogue:

JIM: Everyone else got their fair share of the money and did well by it. As for Ben Gunn, he was back on the streets after three weeks, or, to be exact, nineteen days. And as for Silver we have heard no more. And that's how the story ends. Pretty good, huh?

THE END

Sneak Peeks at other Playing With Plays books:

King Lear for Kids..Pg 99

Three Musketeers for Kids..Pg 102

Sneak peek of
King Lear for Kids
ACT 1 SCENE 1
KING LEAR's palace

(enter FOOL entertaining the audience with jokes, dancing, juggling, Hula Hooping... whatever the actor's skill may be; enter KENT)

KENT: Hey, Fool!

FOOL: What did you call me?!

KENT: I called you Fool.

FOOL: That's my name, don't wear it out! *(to audience)* Seriously, that's my name in the play!

(enter LEAR, CORNWALL, ALBANY, GONERIL, REGAN, and CORDELIA)

LEAR: The lords of France and Burgundy are outside. They both want to marry you, Cordelia.

ALL: Ooooooo!

LEAR: *(to audience)* Between you and me she IS my favorite child! *(to the girls)* Daughters, I need to talk to you about something. It's a really big deal.

GONERIL & REGAN: Did you buy us presents?

LEAR: This is even better than presents!

GONERIL & REGAN: Goody, goody!!!

CORDELIA: Father, your love is enough for me.

LEAR: Give me the map there, Kent. Girls, I'm tired. I've made a decision: Know that we - and by 'we' I mean 'me' - have divided in three our kingdom...

KENT: Whoa! Sir, dividing the kingdom may cause chaos! People could die!

FOOL: Well, this IS a tragedy...

LEAR: You worry too much, Kent. I'm giving it to my daughters so their husbands can be rich and powerful... like me!

CORNWALL & ALBANY: Sweet!

GONERIL & REGAN: Wait... what?

CORDELIA: This is olden times. That means that everything we own belongs to our husbands.

GONERIL & REGAN: Olden times stink!

CORDELIA: Truth.

LEAR: So, my daughters, tell your daddy how much you love him. Goneril, our eldest-born, speak first.

GONERIL: Sir, I love you more than words can say! More than outer space, puppies and cotton candy! I love you more than any child has ever loved a father in the history of the entire world, dearest Pops!

CORDELIA: *(to audience)* Holy moly! Surely, he won't be fooled by that. *(to self)* Love, and be silent.

LEAR: Thanks, sweetie! I'm giving you this big chunk of the kingdom here. What says our second daughter, Our dearest Regan, wife to Cornwall? Speak.

REGAN: What she said, Daddy... times a thousand!

CORDELIA: *(to audience)* What?! I love my father more than either of them. But I can't express it in words. My love's more richer than my tongue.

LEAR: Wow, Regan! You get this big hunk of the kingdom. Cordelia, what can you tell me to get this giant piece of kingdom as your own? Speak.

CORDELIA: Nothing, my lord.

LEAR: Nothing?!?

CORDELIA: Nothing.

LEAR: Come on, now. Nothing will come of nothing.

CORDELIA: I love you as a daughter loves her father.

LEAR: Try a little, harder, sweetie!

CORDELIA: Why are my sisters married if they give you all their love?

LEAR: How did you get so mean?

CORDELIA: Father, I will not insult you by telling you my love is like... as big as a whale.

LEAR: *(getting mad)* Fine. I'll split your share between your sisters.

REGAN, GONERIL, & CORNWALL: Yessss!

KENT: Whoa! Let's all just calm down a minute!

LEAR: Peace, Kent! You don't want to mess with me right now. I told you she was my favorite...

GONERIL & REGAN: What!?

LEAR: ...and she can't even tell me she loves me more than a whale? Nope. Now I'm mad.

KENT: Royal Lear, really...

LEAR: Kent, I'm pretty emotional right now! You better not try to talk me out of this...

KENT: Sir, you're acting ... insane.

Sneak peek of
The Three Musketeers for Kids

(ATHOS and D'ARTAGNAN enter)

ATHOS: Glad you could make it. I have engaged two of my friends as seconds.

D'ARTAGNAN: Seconds?

ATHOS: Yeah, they make sure we fight fair. Oh, here they are now!

(enter ARAMIS and PORTHOS singing, "Bad boys, bad boys, watcha gonna do...")

PORTHOS: Hey! I'm fighting him in an hour. I am going to fight... because...well... I am going to fight!

ARAMIS: And I fight him at two o'clock! Ours is a theological quarrel. *(does a thinking pose)*

D'ARTAGNAN: Yeah, yeah, yeah... I'll get to you soon!

ATHOS: We are the Three Musketeers; Athos, Porthos, and Aramis.

D'ARTAGNAN: Whatever, Ethos, Pathos, and Logos, let's just finish this! *(swords crossed and are about to fight; enter JUSSAC and cardinal's guards)*

PORTHOS: The cardinal's guards! Sheathe your swords, gentlemen.

JUSSAC: Dueling is illegal! You are under arrest!

ARAMIS: *(to ATHOS and PORTHOS)* There are five of them and we are but three.

D'ARTAGNAN: *(steps forward to join them)* It appears to me we are four! I have the spirit; my heart is that of a Musketeer.

PORTHOS: Great! I love fighting!

(Musketeers say "Fight, fight fight!...Fight, fight, fight!" as they are fighting; D'ARTAGNAN fights JUSSAC and it's the big fight; JUSSAC is wounded and exits; the 3 MUSKETEERS cheer)

ATHOS: Well done! Let's go see Treville and the king!

ARAMIS: And we don't have to kill you now!

PORTHOS: And let's get some food, too! I'm hungry!

D'ARTAGNAN: *(to audience)* This is fun!

(ALL exit)

ACT 2 SCENE 1

(enter 3 MUSKETEERS, D'ARTAGNAN, and TREVILLE)

TREVILLE: The king wants to see you, and he's not too happy you killed a few of the cardinal's guards.

(enter KING)

KING: *(yelling)* YOU GUYS HUMILIATED THE CARDINAL'S GUARDS!

ATHOS: Sire, they attacked us!

KING: Oh...Well then, bravo! I hear D'Artagnan beat the cardinal's best swordsman! Brave young man! Here's some money for you. Enjoy! *(hands money to D'ARTAGNAN)*

D'ARTAGNAN: Sweet!

(ALL exit)

ABOUT THE AUTHOR

BRENDAN P. KELSO, came to writing modified Shakespeare scripts when he was taking time off from work to be at home with his newly born son. "It just grew from there". Within months, he was being asked to offer classes in various locations and acting organizations along the Central Coast of California. Originally employed as an engineer, Brendan never thought about writing. However, his unique personality, humor, and love for engaging the kids with The Bard has led him to leave the engineering world and pursue writing as a new adventure in life! He has always believed, "the best way to learn is to have fun!" Brendan makes his home on the Central Coast of California and loves to spend time with his wife and son.

CAST AUTOGRAPHS

Made in the USA
Columbia, SC
09 June 2025